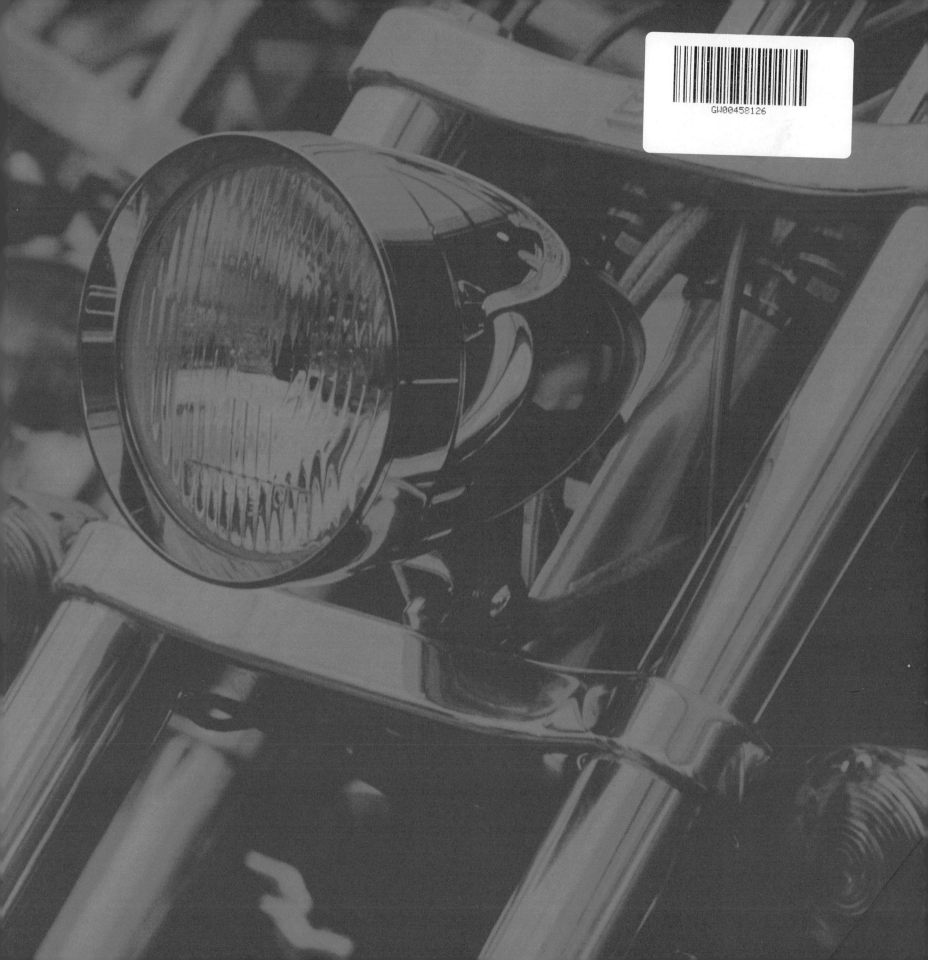

CUSTOM MOTOR CYCLES

Photography by Miquel Tres

Text by Claudia Matheja

images
Publishing

Published in Australia in 2009 by
The Images Publishing Group Pty Ltd
ABN 89 059 734 431
6 Bastow Place, Mulgrave, Victoria 3170, Australia
Tel: +61 3 9561 5544 Fax: +61 3 9561 4860
books@imagespublishing.com
www.imagespublishing.com

Copyright © The Images Publishing Group Pty Ltd 2009
The Images Publishing Group Reference Number: 848

National Library of Australia Cataloguing-in-Publication entry:
Author: Tres, Miquel.
Title: Custom motorcycles / photographer, Miquel Tres.
ISBN: 978 1 86470 355 9 (hbk.)
Subjects: Motorcycles–Customizing–Pictorial works.
              Motorcyclists–Pictorial works.
              Motorcycling–Pictorial works.

Dewey Number: 779.9496292275

Coordinating editor: Andrew Hall

Designed by The Graphic Image Studio Pty Ltd, Mulgrave, Australia
www.tgis.com.au

Digital production by Universal Colour Scanning Ltd., Hong Kong
Printed on 140 gsm GoldEast matt art by Paramount Printing Company Limited Hong Kong

IMAGES has included on its website a page for special notices in relation to this and our other publications. Please visit www.imagespublishing.com.

CONTENTS

SEVERAL YEARS AGO, my wife and I traveled from Spain to the USA to visit several western states. We landed in Denver, Colorado and were met by some friends who are life-long bikers. It so happened that my birthday was during this vacation, and together we realised what better celebration could there be than to rent a big Harley and ride along some of the state's iconic roads. I'd spent my life riding Japanese motorbikes, but a single weekend on a "Fat Boy" was enough for me to understand that this was a different world.

Months later, an envelope with photographs of the adventure reached our home and in it was an invitation from our biker friends to come to Sturgis, South Dakota to take photographs of the greatest biker event in the world—the Black Hills Rally. We returned to the USA in August the following year, and during that week my senses were consumed by the world of custom motorcycles. Wherever I looked, I saw only custom motorcycles. All day long the hoarse rumble of the machines sounded in my ears, I smelled the heady aroma of burnt tires and gasoline, I ran my hands over the bodies of those wonderful machines, and I tasted the beer and the barbecues that are so much a part of the bikers' world. Following this initial experience there have been many more miles and meetings shared with biker friends of all types who embrace the maxim: "Live to ride, ride to live."

It seems that we live in a world dominated by mass-produced products where an object loses a great part of its value once it is purchased and where novelties can become outdated in a matter of weeks or months. However, for a privileged few there exists a strange and fantastic parallel world to which they can escape—a world filled with unique custom-made machines created through the effort and dreams of each proud owner.

The spirit and success of the custom motorcycle world is based on a passion for individuality, the belief in your own creativity, and the courage and strength to go your own way. A core belief in the custom motorcycle community is that the true pleasure of a journey is not the final destination, but the journey itself.

Miquel Tres

ONE PARTICULAR BRAND is synonymous with custom motorcycles: Harley Davidson. It is unlikely that the custom motorcycle world would exist without Harley Davidson. Since the company was established in 1904, it has created legions of enthusiastic fans with a love for powerful machines and the freedom of the open road. These devotees, pushed by a deliberate strategy of loyalty, eventually transformed the Harley Davidson brand into a fully fledged lifestyle for millions of riders worldwide. After some dark years in the mid 1980s when the company was on the brink of bankruptcy, Harley Davidson resurged to become the world's largest manufacturer of custom motorcycles. At present, not only are its motorcycles cult objects, but everything related to the Harley Davidson brand is steeped in almost mythic folklore.

Prior to World War II, Indian Motorcycles was the major competitor to Harley Davidson motorcycles in the USA, and the fans of Indian Motorcycles were just as passionate about the brand and their motorcycles as Harley Davidson owners. Unfortunately, Indian Motorcycles was not able to overcome a drop in sales after World War II and the company was forced to cease production in 1953. In 2004, however, production of the mythical Indian Chief motorcycle recommenced in the company's Kings Mountains plant in North Carolina, signaling the return of this iconic brand.

Other alternatives to Harley Davidson are found among the large Japanese companies and several Korean manufacturers are also tentatively dipping their toes into the world of custom motorcycles. All of these builders attempt to market custom aspects of their motorcycles, but very few can offer the authenticity, originality, and style of Harley Davidson. There is also a variety of smaller companies that produce singular motorcycles, for example Boss Hoss, which manufactures the eight-cylinder, 5700-cc (350-cubic-inch), 1100-pound motorcycles that produce more than 350 horsepower. Despite the wide availability of such alternatives, the Harley Davidson brand has proved so dominant that it will no doubt remain the world's leading maker of motorcycles for many years to come.

Bikes

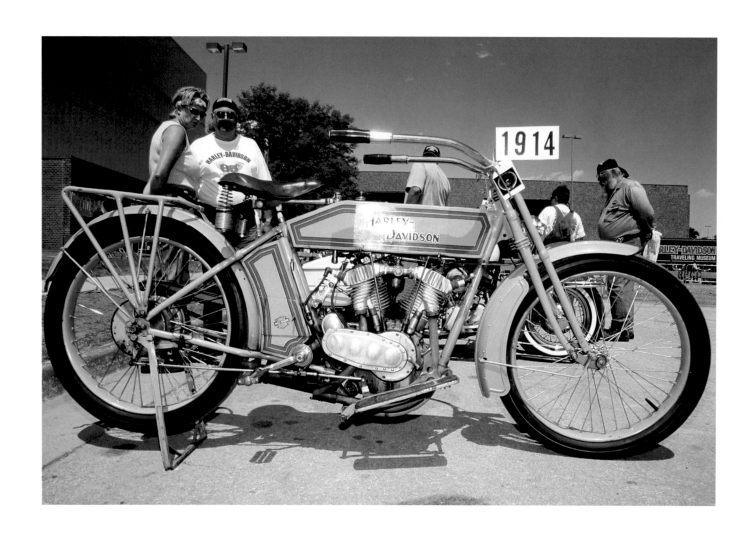

Bikes

Since 1904, Harley Davidson has created legions of enthusiastic fans with a love for powerful machines and the freedom of the open road.

Bikes

Bikes

DAVIDSON

CONNECTION

RR 1000

Buell

POWERED BY / HARLEY-DAVIDSON

1987
BUELL RR1000

Bikes

Bikes

Bikes

Bikes

Bikes

44

Bikes

Bikes

Trikes Another thrilling machine that has similarities to a custom motorcycle is the trike—a hybrid beast that merges the motorcycle with elements of a car. Also known as three-wheeled motorcycles or three wheelers, trikes were originally constructed by joining the rear part of a car (often a VW Beetle) with the front part of a bike. However, with the increased popularity of these machines over the last few decades, they are now usually custom built to specification in much the same way as two-wheel custom motorcycles.

Riding a trike, one is able to enjoy the sensations of a motorcycle with the advantages—and also the inconveniences—of a car. The increased stability means that trikes are safer to ride than two-wheeled motorcycles and are harder to lose control on. Additionally, road hazards such as oil and diesel spills and gravel generally cause fewer problems for these unique and powerful machines. One of the most appealing features of a trike is the ability for both the rider and passengers (sometimes an entire family) to travel in greater comfort. A trike's sturdiness also makes it a great option for people with decreased mobility or who are cautious of two-wheeled motocycles. Yet another advantage is visibility—it's impossible to ride a three-wheeler without attracting attention.

Yet another advantage of a trike is visibility—it's impossible to ride a three-wheeler without attracting attention.

Bikes

Bikes

CUSTOM

DETAILS

MOTORCYCLES

CUSTOM MOTORCYCLE allows its owner to express their personality, freedom, and a sense of national pride. In contrast to other vehicles, custom motorcycles are intended to be unique and fully customizable. The owner is invariably inspired and even obliged to personalize each machine as their own and to distinguish it from others. The high level of customization on these magnificent machines is an extension of one of the custom motorcycle world's unwritten laws—uniformity is discouraged. For bikers, it's important to dedicate a significant amount of time to care for and service their motorcycle, particularly after a long ride. The motorcycle has dedicated time to the biker, so in turn the biker must dedicate time to his machine.

The custom market that enables any biker to personalize a standard motorcycle into their dream road machine is enormous. Common customizations include the brakes, engine, suspension, and exhaust. If in the end the desired accessory can't be found, it is always possible to commission unique parts or even create a special addition with your own hands.

The custom motorcycle world's spirit of independence is also expressed through symbols and graphics, works of art that are found on fuel tanks and all possible surfaces according to the owner's personal taste. Favored symbols and graphics include American Indian heritage and themes associated with the American Wild West; the gothic world and its representations of death in all forms, including skulls and skeletons; patriotism represented by the eagle and the stars and stripes of the American flag; natural elements such as fire, flames, waves, and wild animals; as well as knights and princesses, chains and castles.

Such symbols are not only painted on the machine itself, but are also used to adorn a variety of parts including mirrors, racks, exhausts, rims, and a wide variety of other parts and accessories, including the biker's clothing. Some bikers commission artists and graphic designers to adorn their motorcycles with stunning works of art, while others prefer to infuse the designs with humor. Creativity is one of the basic pillars in the custom motorcycle world, and it's for this reason motorcycle designers play such an ...

important role. The level of skill required to create and assemble a custom motorcycle is truly remarkable. Only the most talented and innovative designers are able to blend form, function, and mind-blowing torque in machines of savage and exquisite beauty. One of the great pioneers in this area of customization is iconic Californian designer Arlen Ness. Since he began working on custom motorcycles in the 1970s, Ness has tirelessly transformed innumerable Harleys into authentic works of art. At present, Ness's company is in the capable hands of Cory Ness, who has recently been joined by a third-generation designer, his son Zach.

Other famous customizers include Mike Corbin, Rick Doss, Rob Finch, Bob Lowe, and Al Reichenbach. Within the Harley Davidson company, Willie G. Davidson has earned considerable acclaim for his work. The grandson of one of the company's founders, Davidson is currently responsible for the design of Harley Davidson motorcycles. More than mechanics or body shop workers, these men are true masters of their craft—designers and artists capable of transforming standard custom motorcycles into awe-inspiring machines.

Details

For bikers, it's important to dedicate a significant amount of time to care for and service their motorcycle, particularly after a long ride.

Details

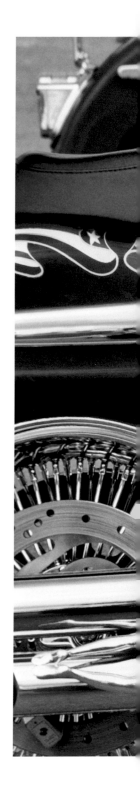

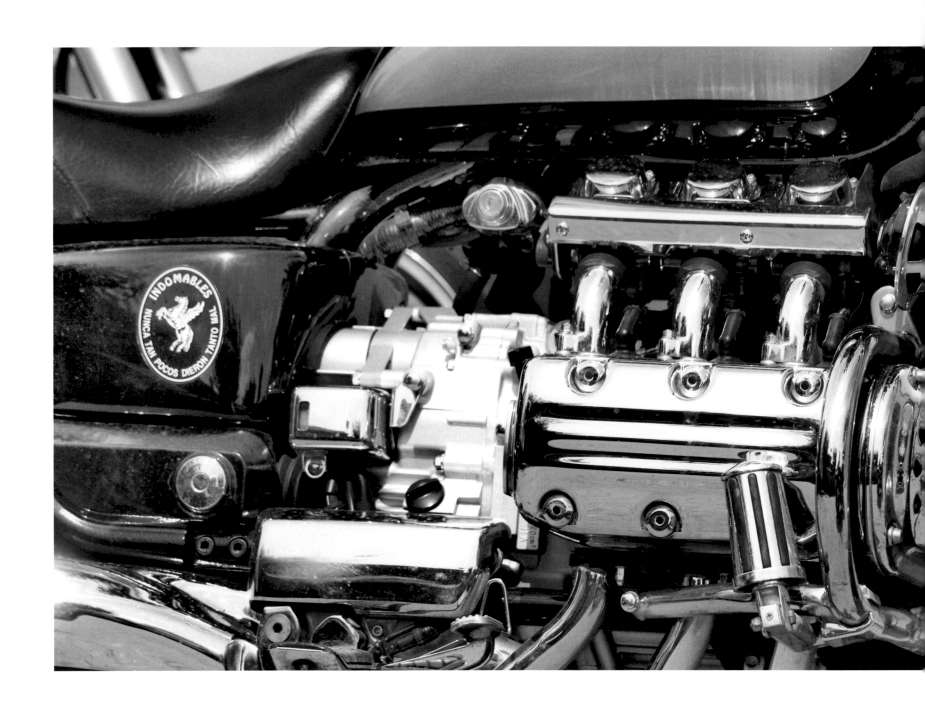

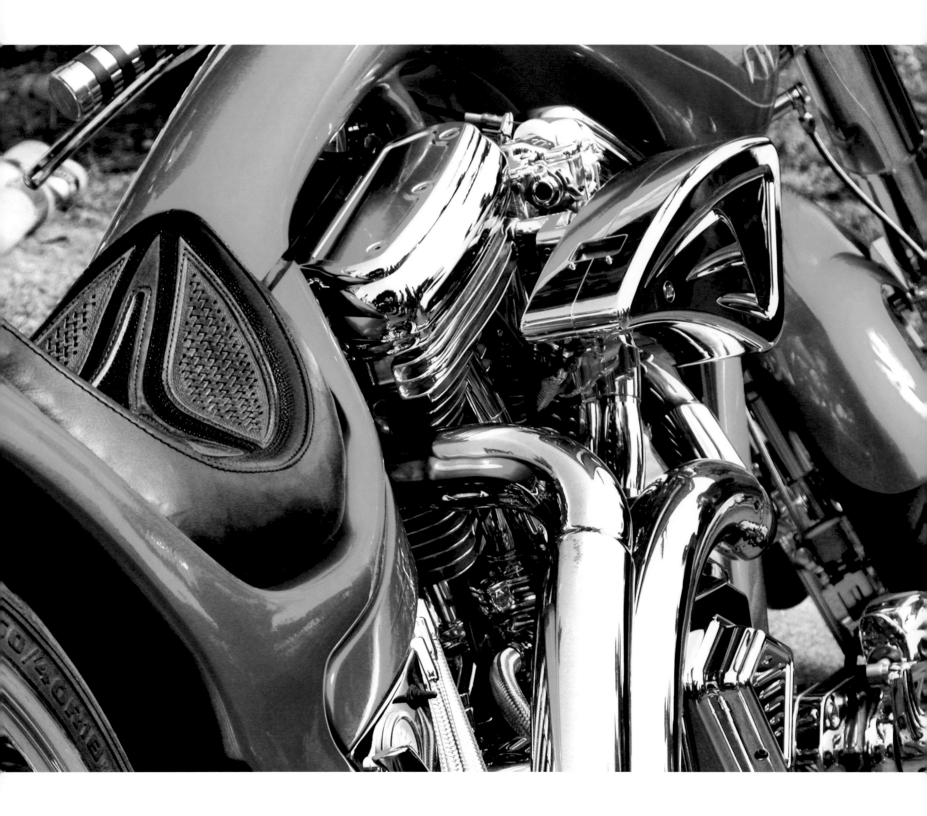

Details 91

Only the most talented and innovative designers are able to blend form, function, and mind-blowing torque in machines of savage and exquisite beauty.

98

Details

Details

Details

In contrast to other vehicles, custom motorcycles are intended to be unique and fully customizable.

Some bikers commission artists and graphic designers to adorn their motorcycles with stunning works of art.

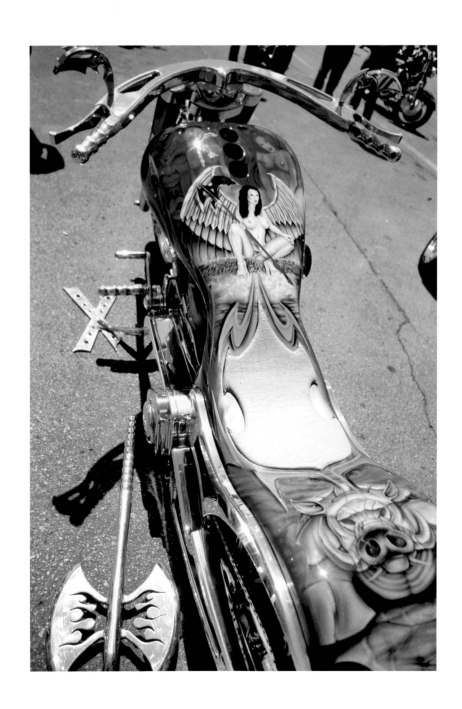

Like horses in the days of the Wild West, motorcycles can be adorned with various accessories such as leather saddlebags and decorative fringes.

Details

CUSTOM

ON THE ROAD

MOTORCYCLES

THE SANITY OF riding a powerful custom motorcycle in dense, built-up urban areas is questionable. Whenever I sit on one of these mighty machines in a city environment, my mind flies away from the city to more remote environments; to places where the miles never seem to end, where your perspective becomes lost on the infinite horizon, and where the road leads to the sunset. Although custom motorcycles are readily found in cities, burning up roads and rattling shopfront windows as they pass by, their true home is the open road—a place where the power of a motorcycle is unleashed with the opening of the throttle, the ride unhindered by the constant traffic of cars and trucks.

Custom motorcycles, much like wild horses, need wide and empty spaces to run and don't like being confined to congested areas. Motorcycles allow bikers the freedom to travel light and fast and provide an unrivaled physical connection to the machine, the road, and the surrounding landscape. An important lesson I've learned is that to enjoy yourself on a motorcycle you don't necessarily have to race through the countryside as if riding a bullet.

It's often better to cruise along, to take your time and fuse with the road, drifting along to the unique sound of the Big Twin beneath you. Riding solo through the landscape is a fantastic feeling, and it could be argued that the sense of total freedom and escape is at its strongest when it's just you and the motorcycle. However, a case could also be made that riding together with mates and sharing the passion is a more intense and enjoyable experience than riding alone.

Such camaraderie among bikers, in which similar values are shared and the same ideals are followed, epitomizes the spirit of the custom motorcycle lifestyle and unites its devotees. No matter the current location or ultimate destination, fond memories of the miles already ridden and expectation of the miles still to be discovered will always live at the bottom of every biker's heart. The exhilaration and sense of freedom that comes from spending days, weeks, even years traversing the landscape on one of these awesome motorcycles is difficult to equal and the bonds and friendships formed during such journeys are long lasting.

On the Road

On the Road

Custom motorcycles, much like wild horses, need wide and empty spaces to run.

On the Road

138

On the Road

On the Road

On the Road

On the Road

Motorcycles allow bikers an unrivaled physical connection to their machine, the road, and the surrounding landscape.

On the Road

On the Road

On the Road

On the Road

On the Road

TO BE A custom biker means being an accepted member of a group that not only owns a custom motorcycle but also follows a particular philosophy of life—one that is intimately connected to and based around every aspect of the motorcycle. A cold beer and a good barbecue—on special occasions an entire pig roasted on a spit—are necessities for biker gatherings, whether large or small. Everywhere around the world there are "in" bars and saloons situated along highways, in towns, or even hidden in mountains where bikers meet to share a beer with their mates, often listening to rock' n' roll rhythms and recalling their past road adventures and exploits. These bars and saloons are often frequented only by bikers, and for this reason such places share a distinctive character suited to the motorcycle lifestyle.

When visiting such establishments, motorcycles are parked outside in designated areas, and if they are Harley Davidsons, in a privileged area marked "Harley parking only." Like horses in the days of the Wild West, motorcycles can be adorned with various accessories such as leather saddlebags with decorative fringes. In many ways, the custom motorcycle rider is the incarnation of the modern cowboy in his leather jacket or vest, proudly showing off his patches that prove his participation in important meetings and gatherings. Other common elements of this biker scene are mechanical bull competitions that embody the dominance of man over beast, as well as the immensely popular spectacles called burnouts.

Burnouts are incredible performances where the owner of a motorcycle—which is often highly customized, very expensive, and in the owner's eyes irreplaceable—speeds up his machine in a closed space while holding the brakes. These amazing displays are characterized by clouds of smoke, noxious fumes, the extreme noise of an engine roaring furiously at high revolutions, and the shouts and cries of excited spectators. Burnouts are performed either as part of a competition, where the bikers are judged on crowd reaction, showmanship, and the overall effect of the trick, or just for the enjoyment of pleasing a crowd. One of the highlights of a burnout is when the tire bursts—the cost is a new tire, but the reward is total respect from all onlookers.

Lifestyle

Everywhere around the world there are "in" bars and saloons situated along highways, in towns, and even hidden in mountains.

Burnouts are incredible performances characterized by clouds of smoke, noxious fumes, and the extreme noise of an engine roaring furiously at high revolutions.

Lifestyle

Lifestyle

CUSTOM

MEETINGS

MOTORCYCLES

ONE OF THE MOST important aspects of custom biker life is sharing a lifestyle with like-minded people. Motorcycle meetings are greatly appreciated by every biker and form a crucial part of their lives. The meetings are opportunities to see and to be seen, to exhibit the latest details, and to meet up with old friends. People ride long distances to attend these events, sometimes crossing several countries or even continents, and sometimes bringing the whole family. For overseas meetings, motorcycles are sometimes shipped weeks in advance, but a real biker should ride most of the way there, thus enabling him or her to wear a patch that says "I rode mine."

The biggest meetings are held in Daytona, Florida and Sturgis, South Dakota, where up to half a million bikers from North America, South America, Europe, and Asia come together for several days and convert these towns into roaring centers filled with custom motorcycle parades, festivals, games, and competitions. The setup is similar whether it's a large national event or a small, local meeting and always includes group rides through cities and the countryside and meals eaten as a group. As night approaches and live music heats up the atmosphere, everyone gets into the mood for celebration and spends the night partying, meeting new people, and recalling past adventures. Once the night hits its stride, people venture onto the dance floor to the sounds of rock, country, or heavy metal music—not surprisingly, many people are still partying at daybreak.

Contrary to popular opinion, very few conflicts or problems arise during these huge congregations of people. Although bikers are sometimes strangers to each other, they share the same passion and show respect for each other. This is because they are united by a common thread— their love for the motorcycle—which for many is the center of their lives and a primary reason for living. Some people on the outside of the motorcycle lifestyle could perceive bikers as intimidating, but this common misunderstanding doesn't take into account the strong friendship and respect between bikers. An important element of these meetings is a code of ethics that ensures the safety of all participants.

Although bikers are sometimes strangers to each other, they share the same passion and show respect for each other.

Meetings

Meetings

Meetings

An important element of these meetings is a code of ethics that ensures the safety of all participants.

Meetings

Meetings

Meetings

One of the most important aspects of custom biker life is sharing a lifestyle with like-minded people.

DURING LARGE MOTORCYCLE gatherings and meetings, events and competitions are an integral part of the celebrations. Perhaps the favorite events at any meeting around the world are the different types of races that take place on a variety of tracks and surfaces, each with specialized motorcycles.

Hill climb In this event, bikers ride up hills on motorcycles that have been specially prepared and modified for improved traction. Some uphill courses have slopes with gradients of more than 45 degrees, and the tracks are often carved into stony or muddy ground. The motorcycles used in such races require a prolonged tilt rear part and extraordinary torque to power up the hills.

Dirt track races Mud track races were originally staged on horse racecourses, but eventually purpose-built racetracks were constructed. Riding in these conditions requires accurate technique because the curves are taken at great speed. The races can be dangerous and riders usually wear steel-capped boots for protection.

Stunts Stunt riding is essentially motorcycle acrobatics. One of the most popular tricks involves the biker riding up on a single wheel—either the front or the rear—holding the balance for as long and far a distance as possible. These stunts are performed by highly skilled and experienced riders, and there is an even more difficult version of this stunt that involves the rider plus a passenger sitting on the front or back of the motorcycle. Although the high level of danger is mitigated by the skill of the rider, it is still an amazing event for spectators.

Dragsters Finally, dragster or drag races are the favorite events for many spectators. These monster machines can be equipped with engines of more than 1300cc (1000+ horsepower) that are propelled by alcohol or nitro methane, enabling them to cover a quarter of a mile in less than six seconds. With riders competing against each other and the clock, these specialized motorcycles can reach speeds of more than 235 miles per hour. These races can be as spectacular as they are noisy and are extremely popular around the world.

Races

These monster dragsters can cover a quarter of a mile in less than six seconds and reach speeds of more than 235 miles an hour.

Races

202

Races

Races

WHO ARE THESE people crazy enough to buy a custom motorcycle, moreover one with a long front fork that is uncomfortable to ride and requires your arms and legs stuck out to the sides? Custom motorcycle owners are both men and women, and although the majority are between the ages of 30 and 50, it is not unusual to find entire families that share this unique passion. Custom motorcycle owners come from all social strata and backgrounds, but buying or creating a custom motorcycle does require a considerable sum of money. There are lawyers and doctors among these custom bikers, but there are also blue collar workers whose main passion—the motorcycle lifestyle—absorbs much of their income and is the focus of all their spending. For all involved, the custom motorcycle lifestyle is no mere hobby—it's a bona fide way of life.

A common element all bikers share is a devotion to their motorcycles, to which they often give undivided attention. This includes long periods of polishing and shining up the chrome and other mechanical parts until every little screw appears to be factory new. A biker always has a cleaning cloth at hand to brush up dirty parts of his motorcycle, and it is this devotion to the care and maintenance of these machines that epitomizes the commitment that bikers have to their unique lifestyle.

Common clothing, such as leather jackets, vests, jeans, sunglasses, caps, as well as tattoos and facial hair among most of the men, goes a long way to concealing any kind of class distinction. But it doesn't matter who you are or where you come from, once you're on a motorcycle and have been accepted by the group everyone is a member of the same "family." Clothing offers bikers the opportunity to display unique patches that show their identity and allegiances and express themselves by wearing specific symbols, emblems, and slogans. Although sometimes this look might appear provocative, it's all part of the biker spirit that promotes a sense of liberty and embraces the desire to escape from the ordinary. Although the style of clothing can differ slightly from state to state and country to country, the long-standing tradition of black leather is a custom destined to endure against all other trends.

The biker spirit promotes a sense of liberty and embraces the desire to escape from the ordinary.

People

People

People

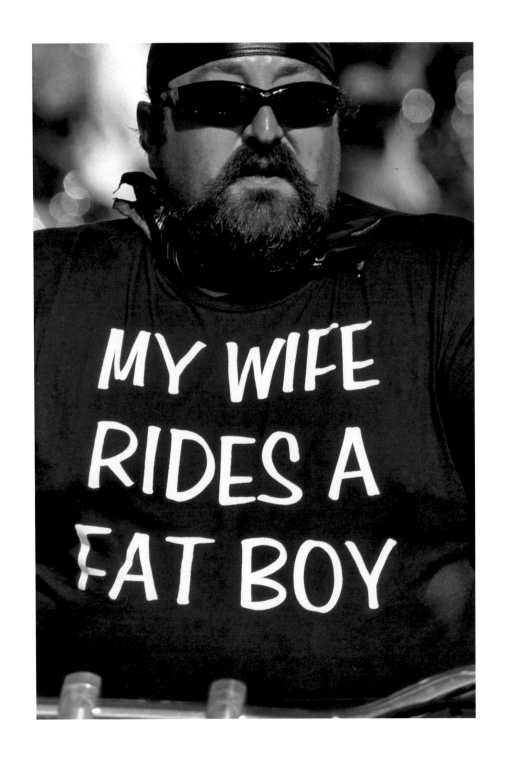

In many ways, the custom motorcycle rider is the incarnation of the modern cowboy in his leather jacket and vest.

People   219

People

People

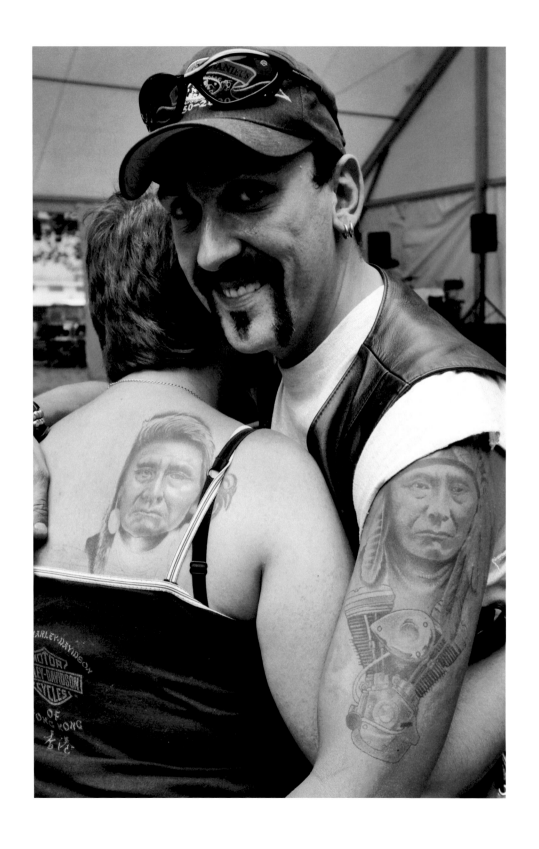

People

For all people involved, this lifestyle is no mere hobby—
it's a bona fide way of life that embraces the maxim:
Live to ride, ride to live.

ACKNOWLEDGMENTS

There are many people that were involved in the research of this book, my heartfelt thanks to you all. In particular, I'd like to thank Pere, Isabel, Claudia, Roman, Ted, Heidi, José Maria, and Eva—all of you are very special people.

I would also like to extend my gratitude to Claudia Matheja for contributing the chapter introductions and to The Images Publishing Group for its assistance in bringing this exciting project to life.

Miquel Tres